The Collector's Se

Perfect

PIES

From Dinner to Dessert

by Polly Clingerman

THE AMERICAN ★COOKING★ GUILD™

Boynton Beach, Florida

Dedication
To Karen Perrino, editor, critic, mentor and friend who has serenely guided and
accompanied me through the joys and travails of these many books.

Acknowledgments
A thank you to Joan's stalwart Lake of the Woods tasting brigade who selflessly ate
their way through passels of pies and crocks of cookies.
—Recipe testing by Joan Patten
—Design and typesetting by Freudenheim Graves
—Illustrations by Jim Haynes

More... Quick Recipes for Creative Cooking!
The American Cooking Guild's *Collector's Series* includes over 30 popular cooking top-
ics such as Barbeque, Breakfasts & Brunches, Chicken, Cookies, Hors d' Oeuvres, Sea-
food, Tea, Coffee, Pasta, Pizza, Salads, Italian and many more. Each book contains more
than 50 selected recipes. For a catalog of these and many other full sized cookbooks,
send $1 to the address below and a coupon will be included for $1 off your first order.

Cookbooks Make Great Premiums!
The American Cooking Guild has been the premier publisher of private label and cus-
tom cookbooks since 1981. Retailers, manufacturers, and food companies have all chosen The American Cooking Guild to publish their premium and promotional cookbooks. For further information on our special markets programs please contact the ad-
dress below.

The American Cooking Guild
3600-K South Congress Avenue
Boynton Beach, FL 33426-8488
1-800-367-9388

Contents

Pie Crusts

Savory Pies

Sweet Pies

Introduction

Pies are part of our folk lore. Something is "as American as Mom's apple pie." When you've put things right, they are in "apple pie order." Heavenly day dreams are "pie in the sky." Jack Horner pulled plums from his pie, someone else baked four and twenty blackbirds in one, and on a summer's day the Queen of Hearts made some tarts. As a child, I knew these had to be strawberry and I longed to taste one.

No wonder we all love to bake pies and feel so good when we roll the dough, heap in the fillings and smell the crust baking to a golden brown.

Baking is magic and bakers are magicians whose fingers turn a little heap of flour and a lump of butter into crumbly flecks and then, with a magical sprinkle of water, conjure the flecks into rags and moments later into a sleek and satiny dough that feels alive under the fingers, a dough that almost sighs under the gentle nudge of the rolling pin.

Out of so little you can create marvels. Flaky crust oozing syrupy fruit, brimming with tart, shimmery lemon or mysterious dark chocolate. Spicy meat mixtures hide beneath crisp pastry jackets. It's magical!

Some of the most seductive of baking's enchantments are the heavenly odors that waft from the oven, filling the house with rich smells of caramelizing sugar, buttery crusts, vanilla, nutmeg, cinnamon and the fruity perfume of apples, cherries and blueberries.

These are the joys that come when you put on your apron and reach for the butter and flour. You are a magician, ready to pull glories out of your chef's hat. Look through these mouth-watering recipes, lick your lips and take up your rolling pin. Let the sorcery begin!

How to Make A Prize-Winning Pie

Pie crust scares beginning cooks who have bought into the myth that making a tender crust requires some special gift or mystic trick. Actually, making tender crusts is simple. Now that we have food processors, it is also quick. Pastry making doesn't take a lot of equipment, but baking is easier and much more fun when you have the right tools in the kitchen.

Equipment

Here is a list of things that will help you turn out perfect pies:

Rolling pin: A large, heavy rolling pin makes it easier to roll out crusts.

Board or canvas cloth: This is the surface used to roll out the dough. Wood and canvas are ideal, but any smooth surface will work, including a clean counter top.

Pastry cutter: Used for cutting in fat. You can also use a fork, or two knives.

Dredger: A large, metal shaker that's handy for dusting flour on the rolling surface.

Dough scraper: This wonderful tool helps gather the dough together. When you lift a rolled crust, the scraper blade slips easily under the dough to detach it from the board. For cleanup, use it to scrape the board or work surface.

Pastry wheel: This looks like a small pizza cutter, and comes with either a straight or a crinkled edge. Useful for cutting strips for lattice crusts and for cutting out pastry rounds to bake separately on a baking sheet.

Pie plates: Crusts bake up crisp and brown in dark metal or ovenproof glass. Shiny metal pans reflect the heat away from the pastry, which hinders browning and crisping.

Ruler: This helps you roll dough to the size you want.

Knife or kitchen scissors: Use to cut off overhanging dough, once the pie crust is placed in the pie plate.

Waxed paper or aluminum foil: For lining crusts that will be baked empty.

Pie weights: Use to weight down the lining when a crust is baked empty. Raw rice or dried beans can also be used.

Pie top cutters: Use pie top cutters to cut decorative designs in the top pie crust.

Pastry brush: Use to brush on glaze, or to brush excess flour off rolled out dough.

Mixing the Dough

The instructions below look long because I tried to anticipate any question you might have once you start mixing, rolling and filling. Glance through them now so you'll know where to go when you need help.

1. Gather your ingredients and tools.

2. Measure the dry ingredients into a mixing bowl.

3. Cut the fat into the flour in marble-size pieces or ½" slices.

4. With the pastry blender, 2 knives used scissors fashion, a fork, or your fingertips, rub or cut the fat until the pieces are the size specified by the recipe. Larger pieces (pea size) make a flaky, crisp pastry that shatters when you bite into it. Smaller ones (the size of bread crumbs or coarse meal) make tender pastry that crumbles when you bite.

5. When you add the ice water, add only two-thirds of what the recipe calls for. Sprinkle it evenly over the flour-fat mixture, mix quickly with a fork and try to gather the dough into a ball. If it crumbles and won't hold together, add more water, a teaspoon at a time.

Cold and Heat Affect Pastry

1. Have Fat and Water Very Cold. Solid vegetable shortening—the sort that comes in a can—may be at room temperature.

2. Chill Dough After Mixing. If you have time, chill it in the refrigerator for 30 minutes. It will be easier to handle, less likely to shrink, and bake up flakier.

3. Use a Hot Oven. High heat explodes solid fat particles (you chill dough to harden the fat). The explosions create steam which lightens and crisps the pastry. At lower oven temperatures, the fat just softens and melts—no explosion, no crisping steam.

6. As soon as the mixture holds together, shape it into one-crust-size balls, flatten them with the palm of your hand and wrap in plastic.

7. Chill for 30 minutes. This allows the flour to completely absorb the moisture so the dough won't shrink in the oven. It also firms up the fat so the dough is easier to handle. Dough can remain up to 3 days in the fridge, or freeze it for up to 3 months.

Mixing Dough in the Food Processor

Many cooks make all their pastry in the food processor. It's as quick as using a mix and so much better. Remember, butter and margarine must be very cold although solid vegetable shortening can be room temperature.

1. Measure ice water into a cup with a pouring lip.

2. Place flour and salt in the processor bowl. Pulse it a couple of times to mix and aerate.

3. Cut butter and/or shortening into ½" cubes and drop them on the flour.

4. Cover and give 4 or 5 quick pulses. Check to see if the texture is what the recipe specifies. If not, keep pulsing, stopping and checking until it is. This step is usually just a matter of seconds.

5. Add two-thirds of the ice water. Give the motor a couple pulses, then add the remaining water a tablespoon at a time, pulsing after each addition. Add water until the dough barely holds together. It should still be a bit crumbly; you don't want it to form a tight ball.

6. Scrape the dough onto wax paper, flatten it into one-crust-size rounds and chill.

Rolling the Dough

1. Let chilled dough warm for a few minutes at room temperature. It's ready to roll out when it gives slightly to finger pressure. Dough that's too cold (or too dry) will crack at the edges when you try to roll it.

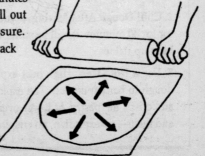

2. Flour the work surface lightly with about 1 tablespoon of flour. A large metal shaker (also called a dredger) is a handy tool for this. Or take a

small handful of flour, hold your hand in the air and fling the flour sideways so it snows down in an even layer.

3. Place the dough on the floured surface and shape a flat, round cake about 1" thick. Place the rolling pin in the center of the dough. With light strokes roll away from you to within ½" of the edge. Give the dough a quarter turn and roll out from the center again—always rolling away from you. Continue turning and rolling until the dough is ¼" to ⅛" thick and its diameter 2" to 3" larger than the pan you will use (10" to 11" in diameter for an 8" pie, and 11" to 12" in diameter for a 9" pie).

Fitting the Dough into the Pan

1. Place the dough in the pie plate. Here are a couple of easy ways to lift dough. Roll it around the rolling pin. Place the pin on the far edge of the pastry. Slide a metal spatula or your dough scraper under the pastry and gradually roll the pin toward you, guiding the pastry so it wraps around the pin loosely. Or fold the dough in quarters and lay it in the pie dish with the point in the center.

2. Unroll or unfold the dough onto the pan.

3. With one hand lift the edges of the pastry and, with the finger of the other hand, ease the dough into the area where pan sides and bottom meet. Press it gently against sides and bottom to insure that no air is trapped between dough and pan to form blisters. Don't stretch the dough or it will retaliate by shrinking back when it bakes.

4. Trim the overhang with a knife or kitchen scissors to 1".

Making a Single Crust Pie

1. Fold the overhanging dough under. Then crimp or flute the thickened rim. You can now put the shell in the refrigerator for up to 3 days or wrap and freeze it. If you chill the shell longer than 30 minutes, cover it well with plastic wrap to prevent it from drying out.

2. Fill and bake as the recipe directs.

Baking an Empty Pie Shell

Pie shells are baked empty when they will have a cold filling such as pudding, a gelatin mixture or chicken salad. They are also used for wet mixtures that will be baked like quiches and custards. A pre-baked shell is less likely to get a soggy bottom.

1. Preheat the oven to 425°.

2. To discourage puffs and blisters in the crust, prick the bottom and sides all over at ¼" intervals with a fork. Line the shell with wax paper or foil, and fill with pie weights, raw rice or dried beans.

3. Bake at 425° for 15 minutes.

4. Remove rice and paper, prick any spots that look like they might puff and return the shell to the oven for 5 minutes or until the bottom looks dry and is only slightly browned if the crust will bake again. Bake until golden if the shell won't bake again. If you use rice or beans, save and reuse.

Glazing Makes It Golden

A glaze won't affect the taste or texture of your crust, but it gives the pie an elegant, golden finish. A glazed finish makes pies look very professional. To make sweet pies tempting, sprinkle the glazed top with granulated sugar before baking.

Before baking the pie, paint the top crust with any of these:

- 1 egg or 1 egg yolk lightly beaten with 1 tablespoon water
- Egg white
- Cream or undiluted evaporated milk

Baking Tart Shells

Follow the instructions for pie shells but use individual tart pans or muffin pans. Individual tart pans are easier to handle if you place them on a baking sheet.

Tarts, which are always served out of their pans, need sturdy walls, so roll the dough a little thicker than for pie, about ¼". Cut the rounds 1" larger in diameter than the top of the tart pan or muffin well. Place dough rounds in each tart pan or muffin well. Small tarts usually don't have a crimped edge. Just even the pastry off at the top of the pan or muffin well. Line the tart shells with waxed paper or foil and fill with pie weights, raw rice or dried beans.

Bake lined tart shells at 425° for 5 to 6 minutes, remove liners and pie weights and bake another 5 to 8 minutes, depending on whether they will be baked again.

Baking a Two Crust Pie

1. Preheat the oven to the specified temperature.

2. Line the pan with pastry as for a single crust pie but trim the overhang to ½" and don't crimp the edge. Place the cooled filling in the shell.

3. Roll the top crust ⅛" thick and 2" larger than the pie pan's top diameter. Drape it over the filling and trim the edges, leaving a 1" overhang.

4. Press the top pastry gently against the bottom pastry rim. Fold both edges under and crimp with fingers or a fork to seal.

5. Slash the crust in several places to let steam escape.

6. Glaze the top crust, if desired, and bake the pie as the recipe directs.

A Quicker Way To Prebake Pie Shells

This works well with most crusts except those made with sour cream and cream cheese. It won't prevent all the puffs and blisters, but the filling will hide small ones. Prick the crust well as for a baked shell. Bake in a 425° oven for 14 to 18 minutes or until either delicately browned or fully golden, depending on whether it will bake again. Check after about 10 minutes. If any spots are starting to puff, prick them and continue baking.

How To Bake a Top-Crust-Only Pie

Deep dish pies use only a top crust. To insure a crisp crust, roll the dough thicker, ¼" to ½". A thin crust may be soggy by the time the pie is baked because of the steaming sauce beneath. Some cooks bake the top crust separately. It's easy to do. Just cut a shape to fit the pie dish, lay it on a baking sheet, prick it all over, paint it with glaze and bake at 425° to 450° for 12 to 15 minutes or until browned and crisp.

The British, who make the world's best meat pies, often bake big, baking-sheet-size rectangles of crust. They cut it in squares and serve one pastry square atop each steaming portion of pie filling. This way everyone gets a generous share of crispy pastry.

When Is My Pie Done?

Double crust pie: When the crust is tan and crisp and the filling is bubbly.

Single crust pie: When the crimped edges of the crust are nicely browned and crisp.

Custard pies like pumpkin: When a knife blade inserted midway between center and rim comes out clean.

Meringue pie: When the meringue looks set and is very light tan with peaks of deeper gold.

When the Crust Needs a Repair

It happens to everyone, even professionals. Crusts tear or have small gaps or holes after you put them in place. It's no big deal and patching is easy. Roll a scrap of dough a little larger than the damaged area. Trim the edges, dampen them with water and place the patch, damp-side-down, over the break. If it's a bottom crust, seal by pressing the edges of the patch gently with your fingers; if it's a top crust, press down with a small ball of dough.

For a Browned Bottom Crust

To insure a brown bottom crust, use dark metal or heatproof glass pans. Shiny pans deflect heat away from the pie so the crust doesn't brown and crisp as well.

The Confident Pie Baker

Here are some of the things that happen to all pie bakers, why they happened, what to do next time, and how to turn the surprises into something good.

If	Next Time You'll Know	The Quick Fix
Crust too hard or tough.	Too much water in dough; too little shortening; handled dough too much; over-rolled the dough.	Lift filling and top out of bottom crust. Serve filling as a pudding with a little top crust on each serving. Top with cream.
Crust shrinks.	Too much shortening; pastry was stretched to make it fit pan.	It will still taste fine, so cover the skimpy edges with something like cream or fruit.
Unfilled crust puffed and bumpy.	Failed to prick unbaked crust; crust baked without being weighted down; oven too cool.	Gently break the pastry bubbles with your fingers and then put in the filling.
Juice leaked out of pie.	Bottom crust pricked (you don't do this for a filled pie); top crust not slashed to let steam escape; top crust not well sealed to lower crust.	Bake fruit pies on a baking sheet to catch the drips.
Soggy bottom crust.	Filling was not cool when put into crust. Pie not baked in lower third of oven.	If really soggy, lift out filling and serve as in first hint.
Crumbly pastry.	Too little water; too much shortening.	Crumbly pies are a bother to serve neatly, but they taste rich and wonderful. Don't apologize.
Edge of crust too brown.	Edge not covered with strip of foil during last 15 minutes of baking. (Do this when you see that it is browning too soon.)	If really burned, cut it off. French pastries never have a raised edge. Disguise if necessary with whipped cream.
Entire top crust browning too fast.	Oven too hot.	Cover loosely with a sheet of foil just a little larger than the pie.

Golden Rules for Prize-Winning Pastry

Use the lightest possible touch.

For super-flaky pastry, cut in fat to the size of small peas.

For tender, crumbly pastry, cut in fat to the size of coarse meal or bread crumbs.

Never knead pie dough! Overworking the dough will make it tough.

Roll dough from the center toward the edge.

Roll most crusts about ⅛" thick and 2" wider than the top diameter of the pie plate.

Tender Crust Tip

Flour toughens pie dough, so when rolling the dough, use as little flour as possible. The rolling pin will enable you to use less flour and give you light, tender pastry.

A Fruit Pie Hint

If a fruit pie is going to be really good, the fruit must be ripe and juicy. This means it's probably going to bubble over in the oven. Our grandmothers handled this problem by setting the pie on a baking sheet so the burned-on mess could be cleaned off that instead of the oven bottom. Then came foil and cooks lined their baking sheet with that. Now you could just throw the gunked up foil away. The latest way is to line the baking sheet with nonstick bakeware liners, which are reusable sheets that can be placed in any bakeware. Your pie can erupt like Vesuvius, but the sugary mess won't burn onto the liner. You wipe it off with a sponge and put it away to use next time.

How to Cut a Pie

Mentally divide the pie into the desired number of pieces before you cut, usually 6 slices from an 8" pie and 8 slices from a 9" pie, depending on the richness of the pie and the size of appetites.

Cut double crust pies with a very sharp knife with a thin blade. To cut single crust pies with sticky fillings, dip the knife in hot water. Cut meringue pies with a sharp knife dipped in water after each cut to keep the meringue from sticking.

How To Freeze Pies and Pie Pastry

Cream, custard and meringue pies don't freeze well. All other pies (and pie doughs) freeze very well, baked or unbaked. Wrap frozen pies securely in foil or plastic film and tape with freezer tape, or seal them in plastic freezer bags. If you use freezer bags, press out all the air to prevent freezer burn. Remember to carefully label and date all packages so the blueberry pie you promised for dessert doesn't begin to smell suspiciously like apples as it bakes.

To Freeze Unbaked Pie Dough:

You can do it in several ways:

1. Flattened, 1-crust-size balls. To use: That, wrapped, in the refrigerator.

2. Rolled-out dough circles. Freeze stacked on a baking sheet with a double layer of wax paper between layers so you can remove one crust without thawing the pile. Place the frozen stack on cardboard and wrap. To use: Thaw at room temperature, fit the crust into a pie pan and continue as recipe directs.

3. Empty pie shells in the pan, baked or unbaked. Freeze in the pie pan until solid. Then wrap. If you have several, stack them with crumpled wax paper between the layers. Store carefully in the freezer or put the stack in a container with rigid sides to guard against breakage

To Use Frozen Unbaked Pie Dough:

Frozen unbaked shells: Bake from the frozen state but add an extra 5 minutes to the recipe's baking time. If you don't line and weight the unbaked crust with rice or beans, prick the shell all over after it has baked 5 minutes.

Frozen baked shells: Thaw at room temperature or thaw in a 350° oven for 10 minutes, then proceed according to recipe directions.

Frozen baked or unbaked shells for fillings that will be baked: Let the shell thaw at room temperature while you make the filling, the proceed according to recipe directions.

Freezing Filled or Main Dish Pies

1. Single crust pies, unbaked: Unbaked pumpkin, winter-squash and sweet-potato pies freeze well. Don't freeze cream or custard pies; they tend to separate. It works best to freeze the uncooked filling and unbaked crust separately. To use: thaw filling and crust, fill the crust and proceed as in the recipe.

2. Single crust pies, baked: Baked cream and custard pies don't freeze well. They weep. To freeze pumpkin, winter-squash and sweet-potato pies, cool, freeze, then wrap in foil, plastic film or place in a plastic freezer bag and squeeze out the air. To thaw, leave at room temperature for 2 hours.

3. Chiffon-type pies: Chiffon pies should be completely set before freezing. Don't add whipped cream topping or meringues until after thawing (freezing makes meringue weep). Freeze unwrapped. Wrap when solid, protecting the fragile tops with a paper plate or aluminum pie plate. To use: Thaw unwrapped in the refrigerator for 1 to 1½ hours

4. Unbaked double-crust pies: Cool completely before freezing, then wrap well. To use: unwrap and thaw at room temperature for 30 minutes. Place in a 350° oven for 30 minutes or until the center is warm. To test, slip a knife blade through a slit, leave it for 30 seconds and feel it.

How Long Will It Keep In The Freezer?

Unbaked dough and pie shells: 3 months

Baked pie shells: 2 months

Baked pies: 2 months

Chiffon pies: 2 months

Unbaked fruit pies: 6 to 8 months

Unbaked main-dish pies: 6 to 8 months

Unbaked pumpkin, squash, sweet potato pies: 4 to 6 months (freeze filling and crust separately).

Pie Crusts

Can't Fail Pie Crust

This is a wonderful crust for the beginning pie baker. You can commit every pastry sin in the book and it will still come out crisp and tender. This one came from a woman who had awful in-law troubles. In fact, the only nice thing she could say about her mother-in-law was that she gave her this recipe, which tells you how good it is.

4 cups all-purpose flour
1 tablespoon sugar (optional)
2 teaspoons salt
1¾ cups vegetable shortening (no substitutes)
1 tablespoon vinegar
1 egg
½ cup ice water

Put flour, sugar and salt in a large bowl. Add the shortening and cut it in until the mixture is crumbly and there are no big lumps of fat.

In a small bowl, use a fork to combine the vinegar, egg and ice water. Add vinegar mixture to the flour mixture and stir with a fork until all ingredients are just moistened and the dough comes together in a ball.

Divide the dough into fourths, each of which will make 1 crust. Put dough you will use now in the refrigerator for 30 minutes to chill and freeze the rest.

Yield: Four 8″ to 9″ crusts or two 10″ crusts

Rich Egg Pastry

Use the method in this recipe as your guide when making doughs in the food processor. This crust is crisp and buttery. The egg makes it a good candidate for quiches and tarts. To mix by hand, see the method on page 7.

2½ cups all-purpose flour
½ teaspoon salt
½ cup (1 stick) very cold butter
½ cup (1 stick) very cold margarine
2 teaspoons lemon juice or white vinegar
1 egg
cold water

Put flour and salt in the bowl of the food processor. Whirl it for a second or two to mix. With the motor off, cut in butter and margarine—about 6 slices per stick. Process with pulses until the fat is in ¼" pieces.

Put the lemon juice and egg in a measuring cup and add enough water to fill it to the half-cup mark. Start the processor and pour in the liquid through the tube. Watch as you pour and stop the minute the dough begins to gather together, about 20 to 30 seconds. The dough doesn't have to form a ball; it should be soft and silken. Turn it out on waxed paper, form it into two balls, wrap in plastic and chill in the refrigerator for 30 minutes.

Yield: Two generous 8" or 9" crusts or one 10" crust

Frozen Dough Is Handy
Keep a plastic bag of 1-crust dough balls or rolled-out crusts in the freezer. It's true that making the dough fresh take less time than thawing out a crust, but you don't have to wash the equipment or deal with the mess.

Basic Butter Pastry

The vegetable shortening tenderizes and makes this crust a little lighter and flakier than all-butter crust, but keeps the rich, buttery taste. If you use margarine instead of butter the texture will be good, but you'll lose the butter flavor.

2 cups all-purpose flour
¼ teaspoon salt
1 teaspoon sugar
¼ cup (½ stick) very cold butter
3 tablespoons solid vegetable shortening
4 to 5 tablespoons ice water

Put flour, salt and sugar in a mixing bowl and mix well. Cut the butter into 8 to 10 slices and drop them on the flour along with the vegetable shortening. Cut in the fat until the mixture is like coarse cornmeal. Add 2 tablespoons of the water and mix quickly with a fork. If the dough is still crumbly, sprinkle on more ice water, a teaspoon at a time, until the dough just holds together.

Gather the dough into a ball. Wrap in plastic wrap and chill for 30 minutes in the refrigerator.

Yield: Two 8″ or 9″ crusts or one 10″ crust

Chocolate Pie Crust

Make the Basic Butter Pastry, adding 2 tablespoons of unsweetened cocoa to the dry ingredients before adding the shortening. This is delicious filled with chocolate pudding. Try it with coconut, strawberry or banana cream pie.

Crispy Pastry Crust

This is a good crust to use for tarts, things like quiches that are presented whole out of the pan or a pie that you eat cold with your fingers. The egg yolk makes it sturdy and adds crumbly tenderness.

2 cups all-purpose flour
¼ teaspoon salt
2 teaspoons sugar
¼ cup (½ stick) very cold butter
2 tablespoons solid vegetable shortening
1 egg yolk
4 to 5 tablespoons ice water

Place flour, salt and sugar in mixing bowl and mix well. Cut the butter into 8 or 10 slices and drop on the flour along with the shortening. Cut in the fat until it is like coarse cornmeal. In a small bowl beat the egg yolk with 3 tablespoons of the water and stir it into the flour mixture with a fork, drawing the mixture toward the center of the bowl as you mix. If the mixture remains crumbly, add a little more of the water, 1 teaspoon at a time. Knead for a few seconds to make a smooth dough. Form two balls, wrap them in plastic and chill for 30 minutes.

Yield: Two 8" or 9" crusts or one 10" crust

Nut Pastry: Substitute ½ cup finely ground almonds, pecans or walnuts for ½ cup of the flour. For a sweeter crust, add ⅓ cup sifted confectioners sugar to the flour.

Sunburst Crust

Here is a pretty and different way to make a two-crust pie. It is often used for fruit pies. Use pastry for a 2-crust pie. Roll it into a circle large enough to make a 2" overhang all round when fitted into the pie plate (14" in diameter for a 9" pie). Drape the dough over the pie pan and pat down the bottom gently. Pour in the filling. Take a scissors and snip an even saw-tooth edge making the points 2" to 3" wide at their base (see illustration). Fold the fancy edge over the filling toward the center. Bake as directed in the recipe, usually 375° for 45 to 50 minutes.

Biscuit Crust

This is the traditional, old-fashioned American pot pie crust our grandmothers made. It is light and moist inside, crunchy and buttery outside. You can use it for one-crust main-dish pies or pre-baked shells for creamed mixtures.

1 cup sifted all-purpose flour
2 teaspoons baking powder
¼ teaspoon salt
¼ cup (½ stick) butter, cut in pieces
¼ cup milk

Preheat oven to 350°.

Into a medium bowl sift the flour, baking powder and salt. Cut in the butter until the mixture resembles cornmeal. Add the milk. Quickly stir and gather the dough into a ball. Use a light hand and quick strokes so you don't overwork and toughen the dough.

Roll to fit the chosen pie plate or the top of a deep pie dish.

To make a partially baked pie shell, roll the dough ¼" thick, line the plate and flute the edges. Prick bottom and sides at close intervals with a fork and bake at 375° for 10 minutes or until the crust begins to color. Remove from the oven and cool. Fill and bake as directed in the recipe—usually 350°. For a fully baked shell bake for another 10 minutes.

Yield: One 8" or 9" single pie crust

Cornmeal Pastry

You don't taste the cornmeal in this crust, but it gives a lovely crisp texture and adds body to the taste. This is especially good for main dish pies.

1½ cups all-purpose flour
⅔ cup cornmeal
¼ teaspoon salt
½ cup solid vegetable shortening
⅓ to ½ cup ice water

In a large bowl combine flour, cornmeal and salt. Cut in the shortening until the mixture resembles coarse crumbs. Sprinkle 1 tablespoon water over part of the mixture and toss gently with a fork. Push it to the side of the bowl and repeat sprinkling and tossing until all dry ingredients are moistened. You'll need anywhere from ⅓ to ½ cup of water.

Form the dough into a ball, wrap and chill for 30 minutes.

Yield: Two 8" or 9" crusts or one 10" crust

Freeform Pie

This is a pretty and unusual way to make a two-crust pie. It is often used for fruit pies. Instead of a top and bottom crust, you make one extra large crust into which you put the filling. Then you fold in the big overhang, leaving a circle of exposed filling.

Roll a 2-crust recipe of dough ¼" thick to 14" in diameter. Place it on a large baking sheet. If the dough hangs over the edge of the sheet that's all right. Place the filling in the center of the dough, leaving a 3" border of uncovered dough all around. Fold the border in toward the center, leaving a circle of filling exposed. Pleat the dough loosely and pinch to seal any cracks. Brush with beaten egg and water, if you want a golden sheen. Bake the pie at 375° for about 45 minutes or until the filling bubbles and the crust is brown. Transfer the baking sheet to a rack and let it cool for about 20 minutes. Slide the pie out onto a big platter and serve warm or at room temperature. You will make an impression! You can also do this in a pie plate.

Oatmeal Pie Shell

This marvelous crust has an almost nutty flavor and the texture is tender, crumbly and crunchy. It's delicious filled with savory salad mixtures like the Oatie Flan filled with hummos on page 39.

1½ cups all-purpose flour
¾ cup quick cooking oatmeal
¼ teaspoon salt
1 tablespoon sugar (optional)
1 teaspoon baking powder
½ teaspoon any dried herb, optional
6 tablespoons solid vegetable shortening
2 tablespoons cold butter
3 to 5 tablespoons ice water

In a bowl mix flour, oatmeal, salt, sugar, baking powder and herbs. Cut in vegetable shortening and butter. Add 3 tablespoons ice water and mix. If it doesn't hold together, add more water, 1 tablespoon at a time. Chill.

Roll the dough on a lightly floured surface about ¼-inch thick. Place in a pie plate. Prick all over with a fork and bake at 375° for 20 to 25 minutes for a partially baked shell. Bake 30 to 35 minutes for a fully baked one.

Yield: one 8", 9" or 10" pie shell

Note: Because of the oatmeal, the dough doesn't hold together quite like other doughs and may break when you fit it in the pie shell. Just push it back together and patch if necessary.

Sour Cream Crust

This is a favorite crust for main dish tarts, turnovers and meat-filled creations. It is very tender and has a delightful flavor.

2 cups all-purpose flour
½ teaspoon salt
12 tablespoons (1½ sticks) cold butter
1 egg
2 to 4 tablespoons sour cream

In a large bowl sift flour and salt. Cut the butter into small pieces, drop it on the flour and cut in until the mixture resembles cornmeal. In a small bowl mix the egg and sour cream together with a fork. Add this to the flour mixture and work it quickly until the dough forms a ball.

Divide in half, wrap in plastic and chill for 1 hour.

Yield: Two 8" or 9" crusts or one 10" pie shell

The Benefits of Egg Doughs

Doughs that include eggs are a little easier to handle than standard flaky pastry. Egg enhances the color and the butter flavor of pastry. Egg doughs are stronger and are especially good for quiches and other wet fillings. They are also a good choice for pies and tarts that are presented out of their pans.

Cream Cheese Pastry

This is tender, a favorite for turnovers and liquid fillings like custard and quiche. The cream cheese gives it a lovely tang and it bakes to a soft golden brown.

1 package (8 ounces) cream cheese, chilled
2 sticks butter, chilled
2 cups all-purpose flour
¼ teaspoon salt

In a medium bowl place cream cheese and butter. Using an electric mixer or wooden spoon, blend completely. (Or use a food processor.) Sift in flour and salt and mix until a dough forms.

Shape into a ball, divide in half, wrap in plastic and chill for 2 hours or more in the refrigerator.

Yield: Two 8" or 9" crusts or one 10" shell

How Many Tart Shells Will My Recipe Make?

When the yields are listed with each recipe they don't include how many tart shells it will make because there are many size tarts. Figure this way: pastry for two 8" or 9" crusts will make 30 tiny tarts, 18 to 20 two-inch tarts, 16 three-inch tarts or 8 four-inch tarts.

Cheddar Crust

This has a lovely cheese flavor. Use it for apple pie, any meat filling, or fill a baked Cheddar shell with something spicy like chili.

2 cups all-purpose flour
½ cup shredded Cheddar cheese
¼ teaspoon salt
⅓ cup vegetable shortening
4 to 5 tablespoons ice water

In a medium bowl mix the flour, shredded Cheddar cheese and salt. With a pastry blender or fork, cut in the vegetable shortening until the pieces are the size of peas. Stir in ice water 1 tablespoon at a time until the dough just holds together.

Yield: Two 8" or 9" pie crusts or one 10" crust

Use a Food Processor

You can make almost any pie crust in the food processor. Just remember, you are using the blade instead of knives or a fork to cut in the fat to the desired consistency. Do it in quick, short bursts so you can get just what you want.

Tortilla Crust

This crust is made with masa harina, the cornmeal used to make tortillas, which is found in the baking aisle of most grocery stores. You will love this crust. It tastes like a thick, tender tortilla and is low in fat. Heap it with chili, taco filling or even creamed salmon. You can use it also as an unbaked crust. Fill and bake it at 400°.

¾ *cup masa harina*
½ *cup all-purpose flour*
2 *teaspoons baking powder*
½ *cup warm water*
2 *tablespoons vegetable oil*

Sift the masa harina, flour and baking powder into a medium bowl. Add water and oil and stir until a soft dough forms. Place the dough on a well-floured surface, pat it into a circle and roll gently to about ⅜ " thick.

Ease the crust into an 8" or 9" pie plate. Make sure it slides well into the area where the sides meet the pan bottom. For a fully baked crust, prick bottom and sides at ¼" intervals. Bake in a 400° oven for 15 to 20 minutes (15 minutes gives a soft, tender crust, 20 minutes a crispy one).

Yield: one 8" or 9" crust

Crumb Crust

Crushed cookies or graham crackers make a delicious sweet crust. Break the cookies or crackers into pieces, seal them in a plastic bag, and crush with a rolling pin.

1½ *cups fine graham cracker crumbs (about 24 squares)*
⅓ *cup butter, melted*
¼ *cup sugar*

Preheat the oven to 350°.

In a medium bowl combine the crumbs, melted butter and sugar. Press the crumb mixture firmly over the bottom and up the sides of a 9" pie pan. Bake for 10 minutes. Cool before using. **Yield:** one 9" crust

Cookie Crumb Crust: instead of graham crackers use crushed gingersnaps, chocolate wafers or vanilla wafers. Omit the sugar.

Nut Crumb Crust: Use 1 cup any crumbs plus ½ cup finely chopped nuts. Omit the sugar if using cookie crumbs.

Savory Pies

Chicken Pot Pie

This tastes like there was a Grandma who loved to cook in the kitchen. Tender chicken and vegetables in an honest, old fashioned gravy with not one trendy, show-off ingredient. This is good with the Basic Butter Pastry or Cheddar Crust.

pastry for a 9" pie crust
5 tablespoons butter or margarine,
    divided
2 tablespoons vegetable oil, divided
10 ounces whole small fresh mushrooms
4 medium leeks, white part only, sliced
    or 2 medium onions
3 large carrots, peeled, sliced thin
2 pounds boneless chicken thighs,
    skinned
6 tablespoons all-purpose flour

3 cups chicken broth
½ cup cream, heavy or light
1 package (10 ounces) frozen peas
4 green onions, sliced
¼ cup chopped parsley
½ teaspoon dried thyme
½ teaspoon salt
¼ teaspoon pepper
1 egg mixed with 1 tablespoon of
    water

Prepare the pastry as directed and chill the dough.

In a Dutch oven over medium high heat melt 2 tablespoons of the butter in 1 tablespoon of the oil. Add the mushrooms and cook until browned, stirring occasionally. Remove the mushrooms with a slotted spoon to a large bowl. Reduce the heat to medium and add 1 tablespoon butter to the pot. Add the leeks and carrots and sauté until crisp-tender, stirring occasionally. Add these to the mushrooms. Return heat to medium high and add the remaining tablespoon of oil and 2 tablespoons of butter. Cut the chicken into 1" pieces and it add to the pot. Sauté over high heat until browned. Add it to the bowl of vegetables.

Lower the heat to medium. Add the flour to the drippings in the pot, stir until smooth and cook until it is bubbly. Gradually whisk in the chicken broth and cream. Cook and stir until it boils, then continue cooking and stirring until thickened, about 5 minutes. Pour it into the bowl of chicken and vegetables. Stir the peas, sliced green onions, parsley, thyme, salt and pepper into the chicken mixture and spoon it into a 9" x 13" baking dish.

Preheat the oven to 400°.

On a lightly floured surface roll out the dough ¼" thick to a 9" x 13" rectangle. Crimp or flute the edges with your fingers to make a pretty rim. Gently lift the crust and place it on top of the warm chicken filling. Brush with the egg-water mixture. Bake at 400° for 50 minutes, or until the crust is golden brown.

Yield: 6 servings

Old-Fashioned Beef Pot Pie

This is a soul soother on a cold winter night. Accompany it with a big green salad and a homey dessert like warm baked apples with cinnamon cream. You can prepare the stew the night before. At baking time, just pop on a crust and your work is done.

pastry for a 9" pie crust
¼ cup vegetable oil
1½ pounds boneless chuck in 1" cubes
1 cup chopped onion
1 clove garlic, minced
½ cup chopped celery
¼ cup all-purpose flour
1 teaspoon salt
½ teaspoon pepper

2½ cups chicken broth
1 small bay leaf
1 teaspoon thyme
1 teaspoon Dijon style mustard
1 teaspoon brown sugar
¼ cup chopped parsley
6 medium red potatoes, in ¾ " to 1" cubes
2 cups carrots, in ½" slices

Prepare the pastry as directed and chill the dough.

In a Dutch oven heat the oil over medium high heat. Brown the meat in batches and remove it to a bowl as it browns. Don't let the pieces touch. When the meat is browned add the onion, garlic and celery to the pan and cook and stir over medium heat for 2 minutes. Add the flour, salt and pepper and stir for a minute. Add chicken broth and stir up any browned flour and juices from the bottom of the pot. Add the bay leaf, thyme, mustard, brown sugar and parsley. Return the meat to the pot along with potatoes and carrots.

Bring to a boil, cover, lower the heat, and simmer gently for 1 hour. Uncover and cook for 30 minutes more or until the beef is tender. Discard bay leaf. Taste and adjust the salt. Cool to lukewarm.

Preheat the oven to 425°. Place the cooled stew in a 2-quart ovenproof casserole.

Roll out the pastry 2" larger than the diameter of the top of the casserole. Drape the pastry over the top. Crimp the edges against the rim of the dish to anchor it. Slash the crust in several places to let the steam escape.

Bake the pie at 425° for 25 to 30 minutes or until the crust is golden. Serve piping hot.

Yield: 4 servings

Hint: The filling for meat pies should always be cool before you put on the pastry. If it is warm, it will soften the shortening in the pastry and the crust won't be as tender and flaky.

Tourtière

A Canadian friend who gave terrific parties always served this luscious, aromatic, double-crust meat pie at Christmas time. It is a traditional French Canadian dish. Use any crust recipe except sour cream pastry.

pastry for two 9" pie crusts
1 tablespoon vegetable oil
1½ cups finely chopped onions
2 cloves garlic, minced
1½ pounds lean ground pork
1 cup chicken broth
½ teaspoon cinnamon
½ teaspoon dried oregano

¼ teaspoon celery seed
⅛ teaspoon ground cloves
½ cup fresh bread crumbs
1 teaspoon salt
freshly ground pepper
2 teaspoons cornstarch
1 egg beaten with 1 tablespoon water

Prepare the pastry as directed and chill the dough.

Heat the oil in a large skillet over medium-low heat. Add the onions and garlic and cook over medium heat until the onions are translucent, about 10 minutes, stirring occasionally.

Add the pork and cook, mashing the meat down with a fork as you stir, until the pinkness is gone. Pour the contents of the skillet into a colander and drain off all fat. Return the meat to the skillet and stir in chicken broth, cinnamon, oregano, celery seed and cloves. Lower the heat and simmer until most of the liquid is absorbed, about 30 minutes. The mixture should be stiff but moist. Stir in the bread crumbs, salt, pepper and cornstarch and let the mixture cool.

Preheat the oven to 425°.

Roll out half the dough ⅛" thick and line a 9" pie plate. Leave a ½" overhang. Spoon the cooled filling into the crust. Roll out the remaining dough. Moisten the rim of the bottom crust. Place the second round of dough on top, leaving a 1" overhang. Fold the edges under, press to seal and flute the rim. Make decorations with pastry scraps if you like. Brush the top of the pie with the egg-water mixture. Lay on any decorations and brush them with egg-water mixture. Cut a few slits in the crust for steam to escape.

Bake at 425° for 10 minutes. Reduce the temperature to 350° and bake for 35 minutes more. After 20 minutes check the pie. If the top is browning too fast, cover it loosely with a piece of aluminum foil. If only the edges are browning fast, cover them with strips of foil.

Yield: 6 to 8 servings

Serving suggestion: Tourtière is generally served at room temperature, but it's also delicious hot. To serve hot, remove from oven and let stand for 15 minutes before cutting. You can assemble the Tourtière up to one day ahead and store it in the refrigerator. Bring it to room temperature before baking.

Double Crust Spinach Pie

This unusual pie, reminiscent of an Italian torta, comes from my friend Meryl who got the recipe when she lived in Nigeria. The combination of spinach, onion, bacon and cheese in a flaky pastry is dynamite. Serve it for lunch or dinner. It will be a family favorite.

pastry for two 9" crusts
8 ounces bacon, cut in 1" pieces
1 tablespoon butter or margarine
2 onions, minced
2 tablespoons all-purpose flour
1 cup milk
3 eggs

1 pound fresh spinach or ½ package
*   frozen, cooked and chopped*
¾ cup cottage cheese
½ cup grated Parmesan cheese
salt and pepper to taste
⅛ teaspoon nutmeg
4 drops hot pepper sauce
1 egg beaten with 1 tablespoon water

Prepare the pastry as directed and chill the dough.

Preheat the oven to 350°.

In a large skillet or in the microwave, cook the bacon until crisp. Drain on paper towels.

In a large saucepan melt the butter and sauté the onion over medium heat until softened, about 5 minutes. Stir in the flour and mix it well with the onions. Add the milk. Cook and stir until thickened. Cool slightly. Beat in the eggs one at a time with a whisk or a wooden spoon. Place the cooked spinach in a sieve and press down to drain well. Add it to the saucepan along with the bacon, cottage cheese and Parmesan cheese. Stir in salt, pepper, nutmeg and hot sauce to taste.

Roll out half of the pastry ⅛" thick and line a 9" pie plate. Spoon in the filling. Roll out the remaining pastry and place it over the filling. Seal top and bottom crusts, crimp the edges and cut slits for steam to escape. For a shiny crust, brush the top with the egg-water mixture.

Bake at 350° for 45 to 60 minutes or until the crust is golden.

Yield: 6 servings.

Zucchini Tart

This is a terrific main or side dish. It's perfect with roast meats and poultry. Try it at your next barbecue. As a main dish, sliced tomatoes topped with fresh basil make a beautiful accompaniment.

1 9" pre-baked pie shell
2 pounds zucchini
1½ teaspoons salt
2 tablespoons butter
½ cup chopped onion
1 clove garlic, minced
2 tablespoons all-purpose flour
½ teaspoon thyme
1 egg
2 tablespoons milk
¾ cup grated Swiss cheese
¼ cup grated Parmesan cheese

Grate the zucchini, sprinkle it with salt and place in a colander to drain for 30 minutes. Over a bowl, squeeze the zucchini by handfuls to remove as much liquid as you can. Save the liquid.

Preheat the oven to 350°.

In a large skillet melt the butter. Add the onion and sauté over medium heat until softened, about 5 minutes. Add the zucchini and garlic and cook and stir for 5 minutes. Add the flour and thyme and cook and stir over medium-low heat for 3 minutes. Stir in the reserved zucchini liquid and cook until thickened. Cool to lukewarm.

In a small bowl beat the egg with the milk. Stir it into the zucchini mixture along with the cheeses. Mix well and pour into the baked pie shell. Bake in a 350° oven until puffed and lightly golden, about 35 minutes.

Yield: 6 servings

Taco Pie

The crust is like a big tender corn tortilla with a soft, delicious texture. It's heaped with a sublime chili seasoned with a hint of chocolate and a bevy of sweet, aromatic spices and topped with spring onions, cheese, avocados. Serve it with more taco accompaniments and you have a winner.

1 pre-baked Tortilla Crust, page 28
1 pound lean ground beef
1 medium onion, chopped
1 green pepper, seeded and chopped
2 cans (16 ounces each) stewed tomatoes
1 can (6 ounces) tomato paste
1 tablespoon chili powder
1½ teaspoons salt
1½ teaspoons ground coriander
1 teaspoon ground cumin
1 teaspoon dried oregano
2 teaspoons wine vinegar (red or white)
½ ounce (½ square) semisweet baking chocolate
2 cloves garlic, minced
1 can (1 pound) kidney beans, drained and rinsed
¾ pound sharp Cheddar cheese, ¾ cup minced green onions, 2 diced avocados, ½ head shredded iceberg lettuce, 1 cup sour cream, as garnishes

In a large heavy pot over medium-high heat, cook ground beef until it is crumbly and the pink color has disappeared. Add the onion and green pepper and sauté and stir until the onions are soft. Stir in the tomatoes, tomato paste, chili powder, salt, coriander, cumin, oregano, vinegar, chocolate and garlic. Add 1½ cups water. Simmer gently, uncovered, for 1½ hours. Stir occasionally. Add the kidney beans and cook for 15 minutes more.

Preheat the oven to 350°. Put the Tortilla Crust into the oven just until warm, about 10 minutes. Pour the hot chili into the warm tortilla shell. Sprinkle the top with some of the cheese, green onions and avocados. Serve the pie with bowls of shredded lettuce, sour cream, cheese, onions and avocados.

Yield: 6 servings

Company Meatloaf In A Crust

When she is suddenly faced with company and wants to serve something quick and dramatic, my artist friend Ellen wraps a meatloaf in biscuit dough and bakes it to a golden elegance. The inside of the crust imbibes the flavorful meat juices while the outside stays crispy. The easy mushroom sauce adds the final touch.

Meatloaf:

1½ pounds ground beef
1 cup fine Italian-style bread crumbs
1 egg
½ cup onion, finely chopped
3 tablespoons catsup
1 teaspoon Worcestershire sauce
1 teaspoon Mixed Salad Herbs (tarragon, basil, marjoram)
1 can (10 ½ ounces) cream of mushroom soup, divided
½ cup milk, divided
1 can (4 ounces) sliced mushrooms, drained, reserve liquid
½ teaspoon salt
pepper, to taste
¼ cup minced fresh parsley

Biscuit Crust:

2½ cups biscuit mix
reserved mushroom liquid plus milk to make ⅔ cup
milk for glazing

Sauce:

¼ teaspoon dried tarragon
1 teaspoon Worcestershire sauce
¼ cup drained chopped pimento
1 tablespoon dry sherry

Preheat the oven to 350°.

In a medium bowl mix the ground beef, bread crumbs, egg, onion, catsup, Worcestershire sauce, salad herbs, ½ cup of the mushroom soup, ¼ cup of the milk, the drained mushrooms, salt, pepper and parsley. In a 9" x 13" ovenproof dish, form the meat into a rectangle 9" long and 4" wide.

For the biscuit top: In a medium bowl mix the biscuit mix and mushroom-milk mixture to a soft dough. Place the dough on a lightly floured board and knead gently 10 times. Roll to a 12" x 8" rectangle. Drape the dough over the meatloaf and tuck the edges in against the loaf all around. Brush with a little milk to glaze. Make three slits across the biscuit top so steam can escape.

Bake at 350° for 75 to 90 minutes. When the loaf is done juices will bubble up in the slits and the internal temperature will be 160°. Test by poking an instant-read meat thermometer through a slit in the pastry. Let the loaf rest for 10 minutes before slicing it.

For the mushroom sauce: While the loaf bakes, make the sauce by placing the remaining mushroom soup in a small saucepan along with the remaining milk, the tarragon, Worcestershire sauce, pimento and sherry. Heat and stir until well blended and smooth. Serve hot with the meat loaf.

Yield: 6 to 8 servings

Bacon and Cheese Quiche

The original quiche Lorraine is just bacon and velvety egg custard in a flaky pastry case, but somehow we have gotten to think of it as having Swiss cheese too, so this recipe has a bit of that. Leave out the cheese sometime and see if you prefer it that way. Quiche is a delicious lunch or supper dish. In small pieces it is a splendid hors d'oeuvre or first course. If you use it for a first course, make it with all whipping cream so it is dense enough for finger food.

1 partially baked 9" pastry shell
6 slices bacon, cut in ½" pieces
1 cup shredded Swiss cheese
2 tablespoons finely minced chives or onion
4 eggs
1 cup milk
1 cup whipping cream
1 tablespoon parsley
¼ teaspoon nutmeg
cayenne pepper

Fry the bacon until crisp and drain on paper towel. Place it in the bottom of the partially baked pie shell. Sprinkle with the shredded Swiss cheese and minced chives or onion.

In a medium bowl beat the eggs slightly. Beat in the milk, cream, parsley, nutmeg and a shake of cayenne pepper. Don't whip the egg mixture briskly and create a lot of foam or your quiche will have air bubbles in it. Pour the mixture over the bacon and cheese.

Bake at 350° for 35 to 45 minutes or until a knife blade inserted 1" from the center comes out clean. Serve warm.

Yield: 6 to 8 servings

Broccoli-Ham Quiche: Replace the bacon with 1 cup chopped, cooked broccoli and 1 cup cubed ham. Top with the cheese. Then pour on the egg mixture and bake as directed.

Shrimp, Tomato and Cheese Flan

Golden, beautiful, cheese-filled and luscious. This pie is a great favorite with guests and it is a dream for the cook because you can prepare crust and filling ahead and put them together and bake just before the guests arrive.

1 unbaked 9" pie crust
2 tablespoons butter
¼ cup chopped onion
¼ cup chopped green pepper
1 tablespoon fresh basil or 1 teaspoon dried
2 tablespoons chives or scallions
1 clove garlic, finely chopped
salt and freshly ground pepper, to taste
1 egg yolk
¼ cup mayonnaise
8 ounces Swiss cheese, grated
2 tomatoes, peeled, seeded, chopped
12 ounces medium shrimp cooked and shelled
3 to 4 tablespoons fresh or dry bread crumbs
paprika, to taste

Preheat oven to 350°.

In a small skillet over medium heat melt the butter. Add the onions, peppers, basil, chives and garlic and sauté until tender, 3 to 4 minutes. Add salt and pepper to taste and remove from heat.

In a medium bowl mix the egg yolk, mayonnaise and cheese.

Stir in the tomatoes, shrimp and cooked vegetables. Spoon the mixture evenly into the unbaked crust. Sprinkle with bread crumbs and paprika. Bake at 350° for 35 to 45 minutes or until the crust rim is brown and the top of the pie has little browned flecks. Let pie sit for 15 minutes before cutting.

Yield: 6 servings

Oatie Flan

This delicious and unusual recipe could be anything from Scotch to Lebanese. The golden hummos topped with parsley, tomato slices and black olives makes a smashing looking dish. Serve it as part of a salad buffet, a mixed hors d'oeuvres lunch, or on its own with cheese and a green salad. It also makes a delicious accompaniment to grilled hamburgers.

1 9" pre-baked Oatmeal Pie Shell, p. 24
2 cans (15 ounces) chick peas, drained and rinsed
1 tablespoon tahini
2 to 3 cloves garlic, crushed
juice of ½ to 1 lemon
2 tablespoons olive oil
2 to 5 tablespoons water
salt and pepper, to taste
2 medium tomatoes, peeled, seeded and chopped
chopped parsley, sliced tomatoes and Kalamata olives, as garnishes

Place the chick peas in a food processor bowl with the tahini, garlic, lemon juice, olive oil and 2 tablespoons of the water. Process until smooth and the consistency of fluffy mashed potatoes. If the hummos is too stiff add 2 or 3 tablespoons more water. Spoon into a medium bowl. Add salt and pepper to taste and fold in the chopped tomatoes.

Pile the hummos filling into the cooled pie shell. Garnish with parsley, sliced tomatoes and black olives. Serve at room temperature.

Yield: 8 servings

La Pizza Express

This recipe comes from France. It's not pizza as we know it, but a thin, crisp crust bubbling with onions, tomatoes, mushrooms, salami and cheese. What's not to like?

1 pre-baked 8" pie shell
3 tablespoons olive oil, divided
3 medium onions, quartered lengthwise and thinly sliced
salt and pepper
4 ounces mushrooms, sliced
4 to 5 tomatoes, peeled, seeded and sliced
1 clove garlic, minced
½ teaspoon thyme
1 bay leaf
½ cup salami or pepperoni, cut into slivers
½ cup mozzarella cheese, grated coarsely
¼ teaspoon dried oregano
halved black olives and parsley sprigs, as garnishes

Preheat the oven to 350°.

In a large skillet, heat 2 tablespoons olive oil over medium-high heat. Add the onions and sauté until limp, 8 to 10 minutes. Salt and pepper lightly and remove them to a bowl.

Add 1 teaspoon olive oil to the skillet and add the mushrooms. Toss and fry until lightly browned, about 5 minutes. Salt and pepper them and add them to the onions. Add 2 teaspoons of oil to the skillet. Add the tomatoes, garlic, thyme and bay leaf. Cook until the tomatoes soften and only about 2 or 3 tablespoons of liquid remain in the pan, 5 to 6 minutes. Salt and pepper them, discard the bay leaf and add the tomatoes to the other vegetables. Fold the salami into the mixture. Cool.

Place half of the vegetable mixture into the baked pie shell. Sprinkle with half the cheese. Top with the remaining vegetables, then the remaining cheese. Sprinkle with oregano.

Bake in a 350° oven for 25 minutes or until the filling is bubbly and the cheese melted. Remove from the oven and garnish with black olives. Let the pie sit for at least 10 minutes before cutting into it. Serve hot.

Yield: 4 to 6 servings

Southwest Sausage Pie

Sausage, a mix of cheeses, roasted red peppers and olives and a tender-crisp cornmeal crust combine to make this hearty pie. Serve it with bowls of salsa and sour cream, with corn and sliced tomatoes, and you've got an exciting dinner that bursts with flavor.

1 pound bulk pork sausage
¼ cup finely chopped onion
1 cup sliced mushrooms
½ cup sliced pitted black olives
¼ cup canned roasted red peppers, diced
2 tablespoons flour
¾ cup shredded mozzarella cheese
¼ cup grated Parmesan cheese
1 recipe cornmeal pastry, page 23
1 egg (optional)

In a large skillet over medium heat, sauté sausage and onion until the sausage is browned and onion tender. Drain off the fat. Stir in the mushrooms, olives, red peppers and flour. Add ½ cup water and cook over medium heat for 5 to 6 minutes, stirring occasionally. Remove the pan from the heat, stir in the cheeses and set aside to cool.

Preheat the oven to 400°.

Divide the pastry in half. On a lightly floured board roll one half to a 12" circle and fit it into a 9" pie plate. Roll out the second half of the pastry to the same size. Place the filling in the pastry-lined pan and top it with the second round.

Cut the pastry to a 1" overhang, turn the edges under and crimp to seal. Cut slits in the crust for steam to escape.

Combine the egg with 1 tablespoon of water and brush it over the crust.

Bake in a 400° oven for 30 minutes or until the crust is golden brown. Let the pie stand for five minutes before cutting.

Yield: 4 servings

Finnish Three-Meat Pie

This is a delectable loaf of mixed meats, onions, mushrooms and cheese encased in a golden, sour cream crust. I got the recipe from the wife of a member of the Finnish Embassy when we lived in Lusaka. She served it with dilled sour cream and lignonberries. If you can't find lignonberries, whole cranberry sauce is a good substitute.

¼ cup oil
3 pounds ground meat (equal parts beef, pork, veal or your own combination)
1 cup chopped mushrooms
½ cup finely chopped onions
⅓ cup finely chopped parsley
1 cup grated Swiss cheese
¼ cup milk
2 eggs
salt and pepper, to taste
1 recipe sour cream crust, page 25, chilled
1 egg mixed with 2 tablespoons milk

Preheat the oven to 375°.

In a large skillet over high heat, heat the oil. Add the meat and cook and stir, breaking it up, until the meat is barely browned. Remove the pan from the heat and pour off the excess fat. Put the meat in a large bowl and add the mushrooms, onions, parsley, cheese, milk and 2 eggs. Add salt and pepper to taste. Mix well. To check the salt, fry a little and taste. Cool completely before you continue.

Cut the chilled dough in half and roll each half into a 7" x 14" rectangle. Place one rectangle on a buttered baking sheet. Shape the meat mixture on the pastry into a narrow loaf that leaves a 1" margin all around. Brush the edge of the pastry with some of the egg-milk mixture.

Roll out the second dough half to the same size as the first, drape it over the loaf and press the edges gently. Seal all around with the tines of the back of a fork. Cut a few short slashes in the top so steam can escape. Brush all over with the remaining egg-milk mixture.

Bake at 375° for 30 to 45 minutes or until the pastry is golden brown.

Yield: 8 to 10 servings

Cornish Pasties

My mother learned to make these flaky meat and vegetable turnovers as a young bride in Michigan's Upper Peninsula, where the recipe had been brought by the iron miners from Cornwall. Pasties were the lunch men traditionally took to the mines. This is wonderful eating! Good for picnics, too, because they don't have to be eaten hot and you can hold one in your hand.

¾ pound sirloin steak or top round steak, in ½" dice
1 large onion, chopped fine
2 medium boiling potatoes, in ½" dice
1 carrot, in ½" dice
1 small turnip, in ½" dice
½ teaspoon thyme or thyme plus savory
salt (about ¾ teaspoon)
pepper
1 recipe Can't Fail Pie Crust, page 18

Preheat the oven to 400°.

Cut the meat into very small pieces—½" dice or less. Place in a medium bowl and mix with the rest of the vegetables. Add salt and pepper to taste.

Divide the dough into 8 pieces. On a lightly floured surface roll each piece to a 6" circle. Heap an equal amount of filling in the center of each circle. Brush the edges with water, then bring opposite edges together over the top and pinch to seal well. Flute the seam with a fork or your fingers to make a pretty edge.

Place pasties on a baking sheet and bake for 20 to 25 minutes or until the crust is browned. Remove from oven and cover with foil. Reduce the heat to 350° and bake for 30 to 35 minutes more.

Serve hot or cold.

Yield: 4 servings (8 individual pasties)

Variation: Make 2 large pasties instead of 8 small ones. After covering with foil, bake for about 60 minutes.

Sweet Pies

Peach Pie

Juicy, sweet peaches with a crunchy caramel nut top. This pie is utterly seductive.

5 to 6 cups sliced peaches
½ to ¾ cup granulated sugar
3 tablespoons cornstarch
a few shakes of nutmeg
⅓ cup brown sugar, packed measure
½ cup all-purpose flour
⅓ cup butter or margarine cut in 5 pieces
1 cup chopped nuts (almonds or pecans)
1 unbaked 9" pie crust
1 egg white
1 tablespoon fresh lemon juice

In a large bowl combine sliced peaches, sugar (the amount you use depends on the sweetness of the peaches), cornstarch and nutmeg. Let mixture stand for 15 minutes to draw out the juices.

Preheat the oven to 400°.

In a medium bowl combine the brown sugar, flour and butter. Stir in the chopped nuts. Set aside.

Lightly brush the bottom and sides of the pie shell with a thin layer of egg white to keep it from getting soggy.

Stir the lemon juice into the peach mixture and pour it into the pie shell. With your fingers, form the brown sugar-butter mixture into little disks and lay them on the peaches to cover the top of the pie completely.

Bake the pie at 400° for 15 minutes. Reduce the temperature to 375° and bake for 30 to 35 minutes more or until the filling is bubbly and the peaches are tender.

Yield: 6 to 8 servings

Country Apple Pie

When they say as American as mom's apple pie, this is the one they're talking about. Probably your mom didn't make it in a Cheddar crust, but you might try it. If you don't use the cheese crust, serve it with a little wedge of sharp Cheddar cheese. Top with ice cream or frozen yogurt, or with a plop of unsweetened whipped cream.

pastry for two 9" crusts
6 cups thinly sliced, peeled, cored tart apples
¾ cup sugar
2 tablespoons all-purpose flour
½ teaspoon nutmeg
¼ teaspoon salt
2 tablespoons butter
2 teaspoons lemon juice
1 egg white
granulated sugar, as a garnish

Preheat the oven to 400°.

On a lightly floured surface roll out half the dough to a 12" circle. Fit into a 9" pie plate and trim the overhang to ½".

In a large bowl toss the apples lightly with the sugar, flour, nutmeg and salt. Spoon the mixture into the pie shell. Dot with butter and sprinkle with the lemon juice.

Roll out remaining pastry to an 11" round and drape it over the pie. Trim the overhang to 1". Turn the edges under and flute to seal. Cut slits in the crust for steam to escape. Brush with egg white and sprinkle the top with granulated sugar.

Bake at 400° for 50 minutes or until the pastry is golden and juices bubble up in the slits.

Yield: 6 to 8 servings

Apple Praline Pie: Make the Country Apple Pie as directed above. Omit egg white-sugar glaze. While the pie bakes, in a small saucepan melt ¼ cup butter. Stir in ½ cup brown sugar and 2 tablespoons cream and bring slowly to a boil. Remove from the heat and stir in ½ cup pecans. Spread over the baked pie and return it to the oven for 5 minutes or until the topping bubbles. Cool for at least 1 hour before cutting.

Blueberry Pie

Blueberry pie tastes of summer vacation, the beach, buzzing flies and lazy afternoons lounging in the sun. This makes a luscious, juicy pie that will romance your tastebuds.

pastry for two 9" crusts
4 cups fresh or frozen unsweetened blueberries
1 tablespoon lemon juice
½ teaspoon grated lemon rind
1 cup sugar
⅛ teaspoon salt
¼ cup all-purpose flour
1 tablespoon butter

Preheat the oven to 425°.

Line a 9" pie pan with pastry. Set aside.

Wash and drain the blueberries. Place them in a large bowl and mix in the lemon juice, lemon rind, sugar, salt and flour. Pour the filling into the lined pie plate. Dot with butter.

Roll out the top crust and place over the filling. Roll under the edges, crimp and slash the top crust in four places so steam can escape. Place the pie on a cookie sheet, in case it bubbles over.

Bake at 425° for 35 to 40 minutes or until crust is golden.

Yield: 6 to 8 servings

Cherry Lattice Pie

Fruit pies are bliss; each bite a fresh, sweet burst of soft fruit and crust that's crisp outside and gooey inside where the syrup oozed into it. If you use frozen cherries you'll need about 20 ounces, if you use canned you'll need 2 cans.

1 cup sugar (use more if the cherries are tart)
3 tablespoons cornstarch
⅛ teaspoon salt
4 to 5 cups pitted sour cherries (fresh, frozen, or canned, drained)
¼ teaspoon almond extract
Pastry for two 9" pie crusts
1½ tablespoons butter (optional)

Preheat oven to 425°.

In a large bowl combine the sugar, cornstarch and salt. Stir in the cherries, mixing well. Add the almond extract and mix again.

Line an 8" or 9" pie plate with pastry. Pour the cherries into the pie crust and dot with butter cut into ¼" bits.

Roll out the top pastry to a 12" round. Cut into lattice strips, each ¼" wide. Lay strips vertically down the center of the pie, 1" apart. Fold back every other strip. Lay a strip horizontally on top of the pie and cover it with the flipped-back vertical strips. Continue adding lattice strips one at a time and gently weave them together to form the top crust (see illustration).

Trim off any excess dough, roll the edges under, crimp and seal.

Place the pie on a baking sheet because it may bubble over. Bake at 425° for 10 minutes. Reduce the heat to 350° and continue to bake for another 30 to 40 minutes or until the pastry is browned and filling is bubbling.

Yield: 6 to 8 servings

French Raspberry Pie

This is pure bliss—crisp buttery crust, velvety pastry cream, and sweet-tart glazed raspberries. Basic Butter Pastry or Rich Egg Pastry are perfect for this elegant filling.

¼ cup sugar
1 tablespoon flour
1 tablespoon cornstarch
2 egg yolks
1 cup milk or half and half
1 teaspoon butter
1 teaspoon vanilla extract
1 baked 9-inch crust (see note below)
1 pint fresh raspberries
1 glass (6 ounce) red currant jelly
Optional: A bowl of whipped cream to accompany the pie

In a small bowl place sugar, flour, cornstarch and egg yolks. Beat on high speed until thick and light lemon colored.

In a 1-quart, heavy bottomed, non-aluminum saucepan heat the milk until it is just under a boil. (You will see a few small bubbles come up the side). Slowly pour about a third of the hot milk into the egg mixture, stirring vigorously as you pour. When it is well mixed, stir the warmed egg mixture back into the pan of milk. Cook, stirring constantly, over low to medium-low heat until the custard is very thick and a few bubbles make their way to the surface. Remove from heat. Stir in butter and vanilla. Lay a piece of plastic wrap over the surface to keep a skin from forming. Cool.

Spoon the cooled custard into the baked tart shell. Top with raspberries, rounded ends up, working from the outside in, in a circular pattern until the surface is covered. In a small pan over very warm heat, melt the jelly, stirring constantly. Spoon the warm jelly over the berries. Chill.

Serve as is or accompanied by a bowl of whipped cream.

*Note: You can bake this in a standard 9-inch pie pan, fluting the crust rim as usual or make a tart like the one on the cover using Rich Egg Pastry and a 9 inch fluted tart or quiche pan with a removable bottom. Drop the rolled-out crust loosely into the pan and press the pastry gently into the pan's contours letting the excess hang over the edge. Remove the overhang by passing the rolling pin across the top of the pan. Bake crust as directed.

Yield: 6 to 8 servings

Almond Pear Pie

This is one of my absolute, all-time favorite pies. Over the years, whenever I announced that dessert was pear pie, diner's faces would fall—until they took that first bite. It was enthusiastic compliments and requests for seconds from that moment on.

pastry for a 9" pie crust
5 Bosc pears, peeled, cored and thickly sliced
6 tablespoons ground almonds
⅓ cup firm butter
1 cup sugar
⅓ cup all-purpose flour
unsweetened whipped cream, as a garnish

Preheat the oven to 400°.

Roll the pastry into a 12" circle and fit it into a pie pan. Set aside.

In a medium bowl mix sliced pears with ground almonds. Heap the fruit in the unbaked pie shell. Cut the butter into small pieces and dot it over the fruit.

In a small bowl mix the sugar and flour and sprinkle it over the pie. Bake in a 400° oven for 15 minutes. Reduce the heat to 350° and bake for 1 hour more. If the edges start to brown too soon, cover them with strips of foil.

Serve with unsweetened whipped cream.

Yield: 6 to 8 servings

Classic Pumpkin Pie

Pumpkin pie must be close textured, soft on the tongue, spicy but not too spicy, sweet but not too sweet. This one is all of that. Sometime try the variations.

2 eggs
2 cups (1 16-ounce can) pumpkin
¾ cup sugar, brown or white
½ teaspoon salt
1 teaspoon cinnamon
½ teaspoon ginger
¼ teaspoon ground cloves
1 can (12 ounces) evaporated milk
1 9" unbaked pie shell
whipped cream, as a garnish

Preheat the oven to 425°.

In a blender or food processor bowl place eggs, pumpkin, sugar, salt, cinnamon, ginger, cloves and evaporated milk. Blend. Pour into the unbaked pie shell. Bake at 425° for 15 minutes. Reduce the temperature to 350° and bake 45 minutes more or until a knife blade inserted 1" from the center comes out clean. Serve cold with whipped cream.

Yield: 6 to 8 servings

Variations: Instead of ground ginger, fold in ¼ cup candied ginger. Or, make as directed above, but add 1 tablespoon brandy.

Caramel Pecan Pumpkin Pie

In a small bowl cream 2 tablespoons butter with ¼ cup brown sugar. Stir in ¼ cup chopped pecans. Press the mixture over the bottom of the unbaked pie shell in an even layer before you add the Classic Pumpkin Pie filling. Bake as directed.

Pumpkin Orange Cream Cheese Pie

Pumpkin pie flavor and cheesecake texture make this a dynamite combination. The light tang of cream cheese blends deliciously with the sweet spices and fragrant orange.

3 packages (3 ounces each) cream cheese, room temperature
¼ cup brown sugar, packed measure
2 eggs plus 1 egg yolk
1 teaspoon cinnamon
¼ teaspoon ginger
¼ teaspoon nutmeg
2 teaspoons grated orange rind
¼ teaspoon vanilla extract
½ cup evaporated milk
1 can (1 pound) pumpkin
2 tablespoons apple jelly
1 tablespoon water
1 can (11 ounces) mandarin oranges, well drained

Preheat the oven to 425°.

In a large bowl, using an electric mixer, beat the cream cheese and sugar until light and fluffy. Beat in the eggs one at a time. Stir in the cinnamon, ginger, nutmeg, orange rind, vanilla extract, evaporated milk and pumpkin. Pour the mixture into the pie shell.

Place the pie in a 425° oven and immediately lower the temperature to 350°. Bake for 35 minutes or until the center is almost set. It shouldn't appear totally set—jiggle it gently to test.

Cool completely on a wire rack.

To garnish, heat the apple jelly and water in a small saucepan, stirring until the jelly melts and is syrupy. Arrange the mandarin orange sections on the pie and glaze them with the warm jelly mixture.

Yield: 8 servings

Cherry Cream Cheese Pie

If you like cherries, if you like cheesecake, if you like them in a buttery crust, you will adore this pie. It's stunning looking with its golden rim, ivory top and glossy red center of cherries.

1 9" unbaked pie shell
1 can (1 pound 5 ounce) cherry pie filling
4 packages (3 ounces) cream cheese, room temperature
½ cup sugar
2 eggs
½ teaspoon vanilla extract
1 cup dairy sour cream

Preheat the oven to 425°

Spread half the cherry pie filling in the pie shell. Reserve the rest of the filling.

Place the half-filled pie in the 425° oven and bake for 15 minutes or until the crust is golden.

While the pie bakes, in a small bowl or food processor beat cream cheese, sugar, eggs and vanilla until smooth.

When the pie has baked for 15 minutes, remove it from the oven. Reduce oven temperature to 350°.

Pour the cream cheese mixture over the hot pie filling and return the pie to the oven for 25 minutes. The filling will be slightly soft in the center. Cool the pie completely on a wire rack.

To serve, beat the sour cream gently with a fork to lighten it and spoon or pipe it around the edge of the pie. Fill the center of the pie with the reserved pie filling.

Yield: 8 servings

Blueberry Cream Cheese Pie: Substitute blueberry pie filling for the cherry pie filling.

Lemon Lover's Pie

If you ever fell in love with the famous Shaker lemon pie with its intensely lemon flavor, this pie is for you. It has the same rich lemony taste but is much easier to make because it uses an extra amount of juice instead of paper-thin sliced lemons. The sugary top crust blends and mellows the lemon's tartness delightfully.

pastry for two 9" crusts
2 teaspoons milk
1 tablespoon granulated sugar
5 lemons, juice and grated rind
5 eggs
1 cup sugar
3 tablespoons butter, melted and cooled

Preheat the oven to 425°.

Roll out half the pastry, and fit into a 9" pie pan. Crimp the edges of the pastry. Line pastry with waxed paper or foil and fill with rice or beans, and bake at 425° for 15 minutes.

While the pie shell is baking, roll out the remaining crust and cut an 8" round (cut around an 8" pie plate or pan lid with a pastry wheel) and prick it with a fork at 1" intervals. Lay the crust on a baking sheet, brush with milk and sprinkle with sugar. Bake in a 425° oven for 10 to 12 minutes or until golden. Remove from oven and reduce heat to 350°.

Using a grater, rub the whole lemons across the small holes to remove the yellow part only. Cut each lemon in half and squeeze out all the juice; remove any seeds from the juice.

In a medium bowl using a whisk or an electric beater, beat the eggs and sugar until well mixed. Add lemon juice and lemon rind. Whisk in the melted butter. Pour into the baked pie shell and bake at 350° for 20 to 25 minutes or until a knife blade inserted 1" from the center comes out clean.

Place on a rack to cool. After 5 minutes lay the separately baked crust on top.

Serve warm or cold, plain or with whipped cream and a drizzle of chocolate syrup.

Yield: 8 servings

Sour Cream Lemon Pie

This has a velvety lemon taste and melts deliciously on your tongue. It looks beautiful with its whipped cream topping and jaunty mint sprigs.

⅔ cup sugar
3 tablespoons cornstarch
1 cup milk
3 egg yolks
1 cup sour cream
¼ cup butter or margarine
1 teaspoon grated lemon peel
¼ cup fresh lemon juice
1 9" baked pie shell
sweetened whipped cream and fresh mint leaves, as a garnish

In a medium saucepan mix sugar and cornstarch. Whisk in the milk. When it is smooth, whisk in the egg yolks and blend well. Place over medium heat and cook and stir for 4 to 5 minutes until a thick custard forms. Don't let the mixture come to a complete boil. Stir in the sour cream, butter, lemon peel and lemon juice. Cool. Pour into the pie shell.

Cover loosely with foil and refrigerate at least 6 hours or up to 2 days.

To serve, garnish the pie with whipped cream and mint sprigs.

Yield: 8 servings

Banana-Cherry Jubilee Pie

Make Banana Cream Pie (page 56), as directed. Drain the syrup from 1 can (16 ounces) dark sweet cherries into a 1 cup measuring cup and add enough water to measure 1 cup. In a small saucepan mix 2 tablespoons sugar and 1 tablespoon cornstarch. Stir in the cherry liquid. Bring the mixture to a boil, stirring, and boil for 3 minutes. Stir in 3 tablespoons kirsch (cherry liqueur) or 2 teaspoons rum extract and the cherries. Cool. Before serving, put a few spoonfuls of cherry mixture in the center of the pie and serve the rest separately as a topping.

Banana Cream Pie

Who doesn't love banana cream pie? It's kids' idea of heaven and adults' favorite temptation. Normally polite people have been known to fight over the last piece of this one.

1 envelope unflavored gelatin
¼ cup cold water
¾ cup sugar
¼ cup cornstarch
½ teaspoon salt
2¾ cups milk
4 egg yolks, slightly beaten
2 tablespoons butter or margarine
1 tablespoon vanilla extract
4 ripe bananas, divided
1 cup whipping cream
1 10" baked pie shell
juice and grated peel 1 lemon
½ cup apple jelly

In a small bowl soften the gelatin in cold water. Set aside.

In a medium saucepan combine sugar, cornstarch and salt. Blend in the milk and egg yolks and cook, stirring often, over low heat until thickened and bubbly, about 20 minutes. Remove the pan from the heat, add the gelatin mixture and stir until it is dissolved. Stir in the butter and vanilla. Lay a piece of wax paper or plastic wrap directly on the surface of the mixture so it won't form a film. Set aside until completely cooled.

Peel and slice 3 of the bananas. Whip the cream. Fold the bananas and whipped cream into the cooled custard. Spoon the mixture into the baked pie shell. Chill in the refrigerator for 4 to 5 hours to set the filling.

To serve, peel and slice the remaining banana and arrange it in the center of the pie.

In a small saucepan, melt the apple jelly with the lemon juice and peel. Spoon or brush it over the bananas to glaze them. Serve immediately.

Yield: 8 servings

Chocolate Almond Raspberry Cream Pie

This is eating! It's a blissfully delicious crustful of chocolate, almond liqueur, raspberries and cream. You don't taste the coffee powder, it just makes the chocolate flavor more intense

2 envelopes (1.3 ounces) whipped topping mix
1½ cups milk
2 packages (4⅛ ounces) chocolate instant pudding and pie filling mix
¼ cup amaretto liqueur or a raspberry liqueur
3 tablespoons unsweetened cocoa powder
1 teaspoon instant coffee powder, dissolved in 2 teaspoons water
1 baked 9" pastry shell
1½ cups fresh or thawed frozen raspberries, divided
1 container (8 ounces) frozen whipped topping, thawed
chocolate shavings, as a garnish

In a medium bowl using an electric mixer, prepare the whipped topping mix according to package directions.

Add milk, pudding mix, amaretto liqueur, cocoa and the coffee-water mixture. Beat for 2 minutes at high speed. Pour into the baked pie shell. Top with 1 cup of the raspberries. (If using thawed, frozen berries, blot them with paper towels to remove excess moisture.)

Top with thawed frozen whipped topping, the remaining raspberries and shaved chocolate. Chill in the refrigerator for at least 4 hours.

Yield: 6 servings

Variation: Strawberries are a delicious substitute for the raspberries.

Fudge Brownie Pie

This moist, chewy, fudgy crustful of chocolate indulgence is the chocolate lover's idea of heaven. The pie will disappear alarmingly fast.

pastry for one 9" pie crust
4 ounces (⅔ cup) semisweet chocolate chips
¼ cup butter or margarine
⅔ cup granulated sugar
¼ cup light brown sugar, packed measure
½ cup milk
¼ cup light corn syrup
1 teaspoon vanilla extract
3 eggs
¼ teaspoon salt
1 cup chopped walnuts
¼ cup chopped walnuts, as a garnish

Roll out the pastry and line a 9" pie pan.

Preheat the oven to 350°.

In a medium saucepan over very low heat warm the chocolate chips and butter until both are just melted. Remove the pan from heat and stir in the granulated sugar, brown sugar, milk, corn syrup, vanilla, eggs and salt. Beat with an electric beater until well blended. Stir in 1 cup chopped walnuts.

Pour into the prepared pie shell. Bake the pie at 350° for 45 to 55 minutes or until puffed. Serve warm or at room temperature topped with whipped cream or vanilla ice cream and a sprinkle of chopped walnuts.

Yield: 8 servings

Chess Tarts

This recipe came from our cook in Nepal back in 1960. He made it as one big pie which he sometimes then covered with whipped cream! Nowadays that seems a bit rich so I make chess tarts instead which we all scarf up with delight. These are wonderful at holiday time.

1 cup granulated sugar
½ cup butter, softened
1 cup chopped walnuts
1 cup chopped dates
2 eggs, slightly beaten
1 tablespoon vanilla extract
6 tablespoons whipping cream
2 tablespoons brandy
pastry for 2 9" pie shells

Preheat the oven to 425°.

In a medium mixing bowl place sugar, butter, walnuts, dates, beaten eggs, vanilla, whipping cream and brandy. Mix with a spoon, using a chopping motion on the butter so that little butter flecks remain after it is mixed up.

Line the tart pans with pastry, trim off any excess dough and crimp or flute the edges decoratively.

Fill each tart pan two-thirds full. Bake tarts at 425° for 10 to 15 minutes.

Yield: about twenty 2" tarts

Chess Pie: Pour the prepared chess filling into an unbaked 9" crust and bake at 350° for 50 minutes.

Apple Cream Pie

This is something different—an open face apple pie. As it bakes the fruit oozes its sweet juice into the thick, cinnamon-perfumed cream. The result is heavenly.

4 cups peeled, cored baking apples, sliced ¼" thick
1 unbaked 9" pie shell
1 cup sugar
3 tablespoons flour
1 cup whipping cream
1 teaspoon grated lemon peel
ground cinnamon

Preheat the oven to 400°.

Place the sliced apples in the pie shell. In a small bowl mix the sugar and flour. Stir in the cream until the mixture is smooth, then pour it over the apples. Sprinkle with cinnamon. Bake at 400° for 10 minutes. Reduce the heat to 375° and bake for 35 to 40 minutes more or until a knife blade inserted 1 inch from the center comes out clean.

If the edges brown too fast, cover them for the last 15 minutes with strips of foil.

Cool on a wire rack. Serve when completely cool, or place in the refrigerator until serving time.

Yield: 6 to 8 servings

Old Fashioned Coconut Pie

This is a chewy, creamy coconut macaroon under a layer of smooth apricot-scented cream. Sometime when you are feeling a bit reckless, drizzle the whole thing with chocolate fudge syrup. Naughty but nice.

1½ cups milk
1 cup sugar
¾ cup shredded coconut
2 eggs, slightly beaten
3 tablespoons flour
1 tablespoon butter or margarine, melted
¼ teaspoon vanilla
1 unbaked 9" pie shell
¼ cup apricot preserves
1 teaspoon vanilla
1 cup cream

Preheat the oven to 350°.

In a large bowl place milk, sugar, coconut, eggs, flour, butter and vanilla and stir to combine well. Pour the mixture into the pie shell. Bake at 350° for 50 minutes or until a knife inserted 1 inch from the center comes out clean.

Cool to room temperature.

In a medium bowl combine the apricot preserves and vanilla. Add the cream and beat until stiff. Spread this over the cooled pie and garnish with more coconut.

Refrigerate any leftovers.

Yield: 8 servings

Pineapple-Lemon Parfait Pie

This delectable, super-quick pie has the tang of a sorbet but the velvety texture of a mousse; the perfect summer dessert. Of course, the richer the ice cream you stir into it, the denser your pie. Guests invariably want this recipe and can't believe how easy it is. Take a look at the luscious variations and then come up with your own.

1 can (20 ounces) crushed pineapple, drained
Drained pineapple liquid plus water to make 1½ cups
1 package (3 ounces) lemon-flavored gelatin
2 cups vanilla ice cream, slightly softened
1 8" baked or crumb pie shell
Whipped cream or frozen whipped topping for garnish

Add water to reserved pineapple juice to make 1½ cups. Place in a saucepan and bring to a boil. Pour it into a medium bowl, add the gelatin and stir until dissolved.

Add the ice cream by spoonfuls (a whisk makes this easy) and stir until each spoonful is melted before adding the next. Refrigerate until the mixture is thickened but not set—5 to 10 minutes (it should mound softly when dropped from a spoon). Fold in 1 cup only of the drained pineapple.

Spoon the filling into the pie shell and refrigerate for 8 hours or overnight, until firm. To serve, garnish with whipped cream or whipped topping.

Variations:

Lemon: Omit pineapple. Use lemon-flavored gelatin. For the liquid use the juice of 1 lemon plus water. Add grated rind of 1 lemon.

Strawberry: Omit pineapple. Use strawberry-flavored gelatin and strawberry ice cream. When softly set fold in 1 cup of sliced fresh or frozen strawberries.

Concord Grape: Omit pineapple. For liquid, use 1¼ cups grape juice plus 3 tablespoons fresh lemon juice and grated rind of 1 orange. For gelatin use 1 envelope (3 teaspoons) unflavored plus ⅓ cup sugar.

Pumpkin: Omit pineapple. For liquid, use 1 cup of water only. Add ½ cup brown sugar, ½ teaspoon ginger, ½ teaspoon cinnamon, ¼ teaspoon nutmeg, ¼ teaspoon salt. For gelatin use 4 teaspoons unflavored. When the filling has set, fold in 1 cup canned pumpkin.

French Apricot Tart

This is light, elegant, and the flavors are divine: a crispy crust painted with a thin layer of jelly, topped with cream cheese, apricot halves and nuts. The combination of buttery crust, smooth cheese, sweet-tart apricots, and crunchy almonds is utterly enchanting.

½ cup red currant jelly (approximately), divided
1 baked 8" pastry crust
1 package (3 ounces) cream cheese
2 tablespoons whipping cream
½ teaspoon vanilla
2 cans (16 ounce) apricot halves, well drained and dried
⅓ cup toasted slivered almonds

In a small saucepan over medium low heat, melt the currant jelly. Beat it well with a fork or small whisk to make it spread easily. With a pastry brush, paint a layer of melted jelly on the baked pie crust.

In a small bowl beat together the cream cheese, whipping cream and vanilla. Spread this mixture in the crust and top with well-drained apricot halves, rounded sides up. Use just enough to completely cover; you will have some left over. Sprinkle with the almonds, then coat everything with a layer of melted jelly. Again, you may have a little left over.

Chill the pie in the refrigerator for 8 hours before serving.

Yield: 6 to 8 servings

Mud Pie

Any pie book should have one dead-easy, wickedly-rich, calories-be-damned concoction that appeals to the little kid in all of us, and here it is: the famous Mud Pie. When life starts ganging up on you, fight back with a slice of this.

¼ cup coffee liqueur (optional)
1 quart coffee ice cream, softened
1 9" crumb crust made with chocolate cookies
1½ cups fudge sauce
Sweetened whipped cream for topping
Slivered almonds, for topping

Fold the coffee liqueur, into the softened ice cream. Heap it in the chocolate crust and freeze until the ice cream is firm. Spread fudge sauce over the top and return it to the freezer for 10 to 12 hours. To serve, garnish with whipped cream and almonds.

Mud pie mavens require that plates and forks be chilled. Since this is a royal splurge, get the details right. Enjoy.

Yield: 6 to 8 servings